SPOKEN ENGLISH

MASTER THE EFFECTIVE COMMUNICATION SKILLS IN ENGLISH

PAILA RAVI SANKAR

To My mother

To My Friends

If you are not willing to learn. No one can help you. If you are determined to learn. No one can stop you.

To have another language is to possess a second soul.

Contents

Prologue

Understand that there is no secret ingredient: Becoming fluent in English – or any language for that matter- is a long-term process. There is no secret super-effective way that can guarantee rapid fluency. There are different methods to learn a language and its effectiveness depends on how well you practice it. Also, different methods suit different people. While some students might prefer informal conversations, others require a well-structured approach. So, if anyone promises you the secret to learning it, don't believe them.

Spoken English is regarded as a passport for assured success in life. The craze for gaining knowledge of spoken English has led to the boom of a variety of teaching institutes all over the country. Much as they may also profess and advertise, it is no longer actually feasible to examine any language in 30 or forty days. An individual who sincerely needs to examine the language desires to spend at least two to three hours every day for at least 5 or six months before he or she feels assured to speak in English. The top goal of this book is to inspire college students to study English as a device of conversation and to allow them to recognize the language thoroughly. This book basically appears at the language from the learners' point of view and guides them through cooperative getting-to-know strategies in order to grasp nice verbal exchange capabilities in English. Each chapter covers one most important vicinity of gaining knowledge of English – defined totally with examples and exclusive interest being given to the simple skills. This book is truly a one-stop answer for mastering English!

ONE
PARTS OF SPEECH

Words are divided into eight parts based on the way a word functions in the formation of a sentence. These eight parts are called Parts of speech.

1. Noun
2. Pronoun
3. Adjective
4. Verb
5. Adverb
6. Preposition
7. Conjunction
8. Interjection

1. Noun: A noun is a naming word. It can be the name of a person, place, or thing. Totally a noun can be the name of anything or everything.

Ex: 1. **Ravi** is a **teacher**.

2. **Tiger** is a cruel **animal**.

3. **Ongole** is a small **city**.

4. **Rose** is a **flower**.

2. Pronoun:

A pronoun is a word used instead of a noun, especially to avoid its repetition.

Ex: 1. **He** is a good boy.

2. **She** plays cricket.

3. **He** can work hard.

4. **She** called me yesterday.

5. **They** are playing with her.

3. Adjective: An adjective is used to describe a noun or a pronoun.

Ex: 1. Krishna is a **kind** person.

2. She is **beautiful**.

3. She is **rich**.

4. I have seen a **strong** man.

5. Tiger is **cruel**.

4. Verb: A verb is either the action or the state of the subject. It describes what the subject does or has.

Ex: 1.Ravi plays cricket(Action)

2. She cooks well(Action)

3. Latha is my neighbour(state)

4. I have a bike(Possession)

5. Adverb: An adverb adds something to the meaning of a verb or an adjective.

Ex: 1.Ram walks **slowly**.

2. Latha is **very** beautiful.

3. I can work **hard**.

4. Don't speak **loudly**.

Note: Most adverbs are formed by adding **'ly'** to adjectives.

6. Preposition: A preposition is used before a noun or a pronoun to show how it is related to the other part of the sentence.

Ex: 1. The tiger jumped **upon** the deer.

2. I prefer coffee **to** tea.

3. Pongal is celebrated **in** January.

7. Conjunction: A conjunction is used to combine two words or sentences.

Ex: 1. Ravi **and** Raji are friends.

2. She is beautiful **but** lazy.

3. Eat something **or** you will die.

8. Interjection: An interjection is a word of emotion. This is used to express some sudden and strong feeling of surprise. There should be an exclamation mark(!) after an interjection.

Ex: 1. **Oh!** She is beautiful.

2. **Hey!** What is this!

3. **Hurrah!** We won the match.

4. **Alas!** She lost her father.

TWO
SENTENCE

A group of words that makes a complete meaning is called a sentence. sentences are divided into four types according to the thought they convey.

1. Assertive or Declarative sentence
2. Interrogative sentence
3. Imperative sentence
4. Exclamatory sentence

1. Assertive or Declarative sentence:

An assertive sentence is a statement. An assertive sentence begins with a capital letter and ends with a full stop(.)

Ex:1. English is a useful language.
2. Krishna is a teacher.
3. Practice makes a man perfect.
4. Radha is waiting for Krishna.

2. Interrogative sentence:

An interrogative sentence is used for asking a question. An interrogative sentence always ends with a question mark. (?)

Ex :1.Can you speak Hindi?
2. Are you waiting for anyone?

3. Whom do you want to meet?

4. Where do you want to go?

5. Where did you go yesterday?

3. Imperative sentence:

An imperative sentence is used for either a command(order) or a request. This is also used to express a piece of advice or suggestion. In imperative sentences the subject 'you' understands but is not found in the sentence.

Ex:1. Do it..(order)

2. Please help me (request)

3. Take care of your health (advice)

4. Exclamatory sentence:

This is used to express a sudden and strong feeling of surprise which may be out of a deep shock or a great joy. There should be an exclamation mark(!) at the end of the sentence.

Ex:1. What a shot that was!

2. How beautiful she is!

3. What a shame it is!

THREE

VERB CLASSIFICATION

1. Helping Verbs

1.1.Auxiliary

i.Be

Is, Am, Are, Was, Were

ii. Do

Does, Do, Did

iii. Have

Have, Has Had

1.2.Modals

Will, shall, can, could, would, etc.

2. Main Verbs

Go, eat, read, write, walk, etc.

FOUR
VERB(BE, DO, HAVE)

Be - Easy Learning Grammar

The verb **be** is used as an auxiliary verb and it can also be used as a main verb. The verb **be** is irregular. It has eight different forms: **be, am, is, are, was, were, being, been**. The present simple and past simple tenses make more changes than those of other verbs.

*I **am** late.*

*We **are** late.*

*You **are** late.*

*You **are**late.*

*He **is** late.*

*They **are** late.*

*I **was** late.*

*We **were** late.*

*You **were**late.*

*You **were**late.*

*She **was** late.*

*They **were** late.*

The present participle is ***being***.

- *He is **being** very helpful these days.*

The past participle is **been**.

- *We have **been** ready for an hour.*
- The present simple tense forms of **be** are often contracted in normal speech. Note that the contracted form of **they are** is spelled **they're**, and **not their** which is the possessive form of *they*.

I'm *here.*
We're *here.*
You're *here.*
You're *here.*
He's *here.*
They're *here.*

Any form of **be** is made negative by adding **not** immediately after it. In the speech, some forms of **be** also have contracted negative forms. Some of these forms emphasize the negative.

emphasizes the negative

*I'm **not** late.*
*You **aren't** late. You're **not** late.*
*He **isn't** late. He's **not** late.*
*We **aren't** late. We're **not** late.*
*They **aren't** late. They're **not** late.*
*I **wasn't** late.*
*You **weren't** late.*
*He **wasn't** late.*
*We **weren't** late.*
*They **weren't** late.*

The major uses of **be** as an auxiliary verb are to form continuous tenses and the passive.

- **Continuous** tenses of main verbs use the appropriate form of *be*, present or past, followed by the present participle (or-*ing* form).
- The **passive** form of a main verb uses the appropriate form of *be* followed by the past participle.

The verb*be* is also used as a main verb. It is commonly found joining a subject to its complement.

As a **main verb**, *be* is used to talk about:

- Feelings and states. For this we use the simple tenses of the verb with a suitable adjective.

- *I **am delighted** with the news but he **is not happy**.*
- *She **was busy** so she **was not able**to see me.*

- People's behaviour. For this we use the continuous tenses of the verb with a suitable adjective.

- *I**am not being** slow, I **am being**careful.*
- *You **were being** very rude to your mum when I came downstairs.*

- *Be* + the *to* **infinitive** is sometimes used to refer to future time. This is a rather formal use, which often appears in news reports.
- *The Prime Minister**is to visit** Hungary in October.*

- *The Archbishop **is to have** talks with the Pope next month.*

- *It* + *be*: we use*it* as a subject when we are talking about time, distance, weather, or cost. In this use,*be* is always singular.

- *Hurry up, **it's eight thirty**!*
- ***Is it**? I didn't know it was so late.*

- ***It's** thirty miles to Glasgow.*
- *Come and visit us. **It's not** very far.*

- ***It's** cold today but **it isn't** wet.*

- ***It's** very expensive to live in London.*

- **There + is/are** is used to talk about something existing. In this use, the form that **be** takes may **be** singular or plural, depending on the number of the noun, and *be* is sometimes contracted.

- **There's** *a spare toothbrush in the cupboard.*
- **There was***a cold wind blowing.*
- **There isn't***enough petrol for the journey.*
- **There are***several petrol stations on the way,* **aren't there?**

To make the continuous tenses of the main verb *be* we have to use *be* twice, once as an auxiliary and once as a main verb.

- *You **are being**so annoying!*
- *I know I **am being**silly, but I am frightened.*

The question form of clauses with the verb **be** in them is made by putting the appropriate form of**be** right in front of the subject.

- **Are you** *better now?*
- **Is he***free this morning?*

- *Was he cooking dinner when you arrived?*

Have - Easy Learning Grammar

The verb **have** is used as an auxiliary verb

- *She**has**run a lovely, deep, bubble bath.*
- *Katie **had** read about the concert in the newspaper.*

and also as a main verb.

*She is **having**a bath at the moment.*

*The driver has**had** his**breakfast, so we can go.*

The verb *have* has the forms: **have, has, having, had**. The base form of the verb is **have**. The present participle is **having**. The past tense and past participle form is **had**.

- The present and past forms are often contracted in everyday speech, especially when **have** is being used as an auxiliary verb.

The contracted forms are:

have = **'ve** *I've seen the Queen.*

has = **'s** *He's gone on holiday.*

Ian's behaved badly.

had = **'d** *You'd better go home.*

Ian'd left them behind.

The form **have** contracts to **'ve**. This can sound rather like *of*, especially after other auxiliary verbs.

- *She **would've** given you something to eat.*
- *You **could've**stayed the night with us.*
- *If he'd asked, I **might've** lent him my car.*

Avoid the common mistake of writing *of* in this case.

As an **auxiliary** verb, *have* is used to make the **perfect tenses** of main verbs.

The **perfect** tenses of main verbs use the appropriate form of *have*, present or past, followed by the past participle.

*I **have read** some really good books over the holidays.*

* *I **had seen** the film before.*

The negative of a clause containing a compound verb with ***have*** is made by adding ***not*** or another negative word immediately after the appropriate form of ***have.*** In speech, some forms of ***have*** also have contracted negative forms.

* *I **have never seen** such luxury.*
* *Rachel **had not been** abroad before.*
* *She **had hardly had** time to eat when Paul arrived.*

* present tense and past tense forms that emphasize the negative element:

  *I/we/you/they'**ve not**;*
  *he/she/it'**s not***
  *I/we/you/he/she/it /they'**d not***

* *She'**s not** told me about it yet.*
* *We'**venot**been here before.*
* *They'**d not**seen him for weeks.*

* present tense and past tense negative forms that are used less emphatically:

  *I/we/you/they **haven't**;*
  *he/she/it **hasn't***

I/we/you/he/she/it /they **hadn't**

- *He* **hasn't** *found anywhere to stay this holiday.*
- *We* **haven't** *been here before.*
- *They* **hadn't** *looked very hard, in my opinion.*

As a **main verb**, *have* is used to talk about:

- states or conditions, such as possession or relationship.

- In these uses, continuous tenses are not possible. With this meaning **have** is sometimes used alone, adding only **not** to make negatives, and adding nothing to make questions.

- *I* **have** *something for you.*
- *We* **haven't** *anything for you today.*
- **Have you** *no sense of shame?*
- *The driver* **has had** *his breakfast, so we can go.*
- *We* **had** *a good time.*

It is also often used with forms of **do** to make negatives and questions.

- **Do you have** *a pen?*
- **Does she have** *my umbrella?*
- **She doesn't have** *any brothers or sisters.*
- **Do you have** *time to see me now?*

- **Have got** is an informal form of this main verb use of *have*, often used in speaking, especially in British English.

- *I **haven't got** any brothers or sisters.*
- ***Has she got** my umbrella? – Yes, she has.*
- ***She hasn't got** any money.*

- activities, including those such as eating, and leisure.

With this meaning of **have**, negatives and questions are formed using one of the forms of **do**.

- ***He was having**a shower when I phoned.*

- *I'm **having**lunch at twelve o'clock.*
- *Come and **have** a sandwich with me,*
- *No thanks. I **don't**usually have lunch.*

- *He's **having** a day off.*
- ***Did** you **have** a good holiday?*

Contractions and weak forms are not possible with this meaning.
Have got is not used with this meaning.

- to express obligation using **have to** or **have got to**.

- ***I've got to** go now, I'm afraid.*
- ***Do you have**to leave so soon?*
- ***Have you got to**leave so soon?*

When **have** is a main verb, it makes perfect forms like all other main verbs. This means that it is possible to use **have** twice in present or past perfect sentences, once as an auxiliary verb and once as a main verb.

- We **have had**enough, thank you.
- They **had**already **had** several warnings.

Do - Easy Learning Grammar

The verb**do** is used as an auxiliary verb.

I **do not** want it. We **do not** want it.

You **do not** want it. You **do not** want it.

He **does not** want it. They **do not** want it.

I **did not** want it. We **did not** want it.

You **did not** want it. You **did not** want it.

She **did not** want it. They **did not** want it.

It can also be used as a main verb. When *do* is used as an auxiliary verb it is a **supporting verb**. Because a main verb cannot combine directly with negatives or make questions, **do** is used to support the main verb.

- **Don't**talk!
- **Don't**run!

It is also used to stand in for another verb to avoid repetition.

The verb **do** is irregular. It has five different forms: **do, does, doing, did, done**. The base form of the verb is **do**. The past simple form, **did**, is the same throughout. The present participle is **doing**. The past participle is **done**.

The present simple tense **do** and the past simple tense **did** can be used as an auxiliary verb. As an auxiliary, **do** is not used with **modal** verbs.

I **do**not want it. We **do**not want it.

You **do**not want it. You **do**not want it.

He **does** not want it. They **do** not want it.

I **did** not want it. We **did**not want it.

You **did** not want it. You **did**not want it.

*She **did** not want it. They **did**not want it.*
As an **auxiliary** verb **do** is used in the following ways:

- to help make the negative and question forms of present simple and past simple tenses.

- *Oh dear, I **didn't feed**the cat this morning.*
- ***Do**you **know**what time it is?*
- ***Did**Tim **pay**for his ticket last night?*

- to make the negative form of a command.

- ***Don't**talk!*
- ***Don't**run!*

- to make a command more persuasive.
- ***Do**let me see it!*

- to avoid repeating a main verb in additions, commands, sentence tags, and short answers.

- *They often go to the cinema, **and so do**we.*

- *Don't run on the road! Don't **do**it!*

- *You live in Glasgow, **don't**you?*

- *Do you play cricket? – No, **I**don't.*
- *Did they tell you the news? – Yes, they **did**.*
- *Jim likes jazz, I think. Yes, **he does**.*

- in comparisons.

- *She **sings**better than I **do**.*

The positive forms of **do** cannot be contracted. In speech, the negative has contracted forms.

- *I **don't**(do not) agree with you.*
- *She **doesn't**(does not) live here now.*
- *They **didn't**(did not) buy any food.*

- present tense negative forms:
  *I/we/you/they **don't**; he/she/it **doesn't***
- past tense negative form:
  *I/we/you/he/she/it/they **didn't***

When **do** is the main verb, it has a range of meanings that includes *carry out*, *perform*, *fix*, or *provide*. It is sometimes used in place of a more specific verb.

- *I'll **do**the lawn now.*
- *(I'll **mow**the lawn now.)*
- *I'll **do**you.*
- *(I'll **punch**you.)*
- *We don't **do**coach parties.*
- *(We don't **serve**coach parties.)*

It is then used with the full range of tenses and forms.
***Are**you **doing**your homework?*
*You **have been doing**well this term.*
*She **had done**enough, so she stopped.*
*This **has been done**before.*
The main verb use of **do** can be used to talk about:

- habits.

- *I **do**the washing up every evening.*
- *This is what I usually **do**.*

- behavior.

- *He **did** something rather foolish.*
- *I **didn't do**anything wrong.*
- *What **are**you **doing**?*

- plans.

- *What **are**you **doing**on Sunday?*

As a main verb, **do** makes negatives and questions like all other main verbs:

- in the present simple tense with auxiliary **do**.

- *What **does**he **do**for a living?*
- ***Do**I **do**it this way?*
- *No, you **don't do**it like that at all.*

- in the past simple tense with auxiliary **did**.

- ***Did**Henry **do**it, then?*
- ***Didn't**Henry **do**it, then?*
- *He **didn't do** it, you know.*

This means that it is possible to use **do** twice in negative and interrogative sentences; once as an auxiliary verb and once as a main verb.

- As a main verb, **do** can be used with modal verbs.

- *They will **do** it for you if you ask nicely.*
- *I can **do** it, but I **shouldn't do**it.*

FIVE

MODAL VERBS

Here's a list of the modal verbs in English:
can,could,may,might,will
would, must, shall, should, ought to
Modals are different form normal verbs:
1: They don't use an 's' for the third person singular.
2: They make questions by inversion ('she can go' becomes 'can she go?'). She could reach in time = Could she reach in time?
3: They are followed directly by the infinitive of another verb (without 'to').
Probability:
First, they can be used when we want to say how sure we are that something happened/is happening / will happen. We often call these 'modals of deduction' or 'speculation' or 'certainty' or 'probability'.
For example:

- It's snowing, so it **must be** very cold outside.
- I don't know where John is. He **could miss** the train.
- This bill **can not be** right. £200 for two cups of coffee!

Ability

We use 'can' and 'could' to talk about a skill or ability. For example:

- She **can speak** six languages.
- My grandfather **could play** golf very well.
- I **can't drive.**

Obligation and Advice

We can use verbs such as 'must' or 'should' to say when something is necessary or unnecessary or to give advice.

For example:

- Children **must do** their homework.
- We **have to wear** a uniform at work.
- He has to wear a uniform.
- You **should stop** smoking.
- We ought to respect our elders.

Permission

We can use verbs such as 'can', 'could', and 'may' to ask for and give permission. We also use modal verbs to say something is not allowed.

For example:

- **Could I leave** early today, please?
- You **may not use** the car tonight.
- **Can we swim** in the lake?
- Would you like a cup of coffee?

Habits

We can use 'will' and 'would' to talk about habits or things we usually do or did in the past.

For example:

- When I lived in Italy, we **would** often **eat** in the restaurant next to my flat.
- John **will** always **be** late!
- If I would have been in your place, I could/would do this.

MODALS IN THE PAST

Could have, should have, would have

These past modal verbs are all used hypothetically, to talk about things that didn't really happen in the past.

Could have + past participle

1: **Could have + past participle** means that something was possible in the past, or you had the ability to do something in the past, but that you didn't do it.

- I could have stayed up late, but I decided to go to bed early.
- They could have won the race, but they didn't try hard enough.
- Julie could have bought the book, but she borrowed it from the library instead.
- He could have studied harder, but he was too lazy and that's why he failed the exam.

Couldn't have + past participle means that something wasn't possible in the past, even if you had wanted to do it.

- I couldn't have arrived any earlier. There was a terrible traffic jam (= it was impossible for me to have arrived any earlier).
- He couldn't have passed the exam, even if he had studied harder. It's a really, really difficult exam.

2: We use **could have + past participle** when we want to make a guess about something that happened in the past. In this case, we don't know if what we're saying is true or not true. We're just talking about our opinion of what maybe happened.

Why is John late?

- He could get stuck in traffic.
- He could forget that we were meeting today.
- He could oversleep.
- He could miss the train.

We can also choose to use **might have + past participle** to mean the same thing:

- He might have got stuck in traffic.
- He might have forgotten that we were meeting today.
- He might have overslept.

Should have + past participle

1: **Should have + past participle** can mean something that would have been a good idea, but that you didn't do it. It's like giving advice about the past when you say it to someone else, or regretting what you did or didn't do when you're talking about yourself.

Shouldn't have + past participle means that something wasn't a good idea, but you did it anyway.

- I should have studied harder! (= I didn't study very hard and so I failed the exam. I'm sorry about this now.)
- I should have gone to bed early. (= I didn't go to bed early and now I'm tired).

- I shouldn't have eaten so much cake! (= I did eat a lot of cake and now I don't feel good.)
- You should have called me when you arrived (= you didn't call me and I was worried. I wish that you had called me).
- John should have left early, then he wouldn't have missed the plane (= but he didn't leave early and so he did miss the plane).

2: We can also use **should have + past participle** to talk about something that, if everything is normal and okay, we think has already happened. But we're not certain that everything is fine, so we use 'should have' and not the present perfect or past simple. It's often used with 'by now'.

- His plane should/would have arrived by now (= if everything is fine, the plane has arrived).
- John should/would have finished work by now (= if everything is normal, John has finished work).

We can also use this to talk about something that would have happened if everything was fine but hasn't happened.

- Lucy should have arrived by now, but she hasn't.

Would have + past participle
1: Part of the **third conditional**.

- If I had enough money, I would have bought a car (but I didn't have enough money, so I didn't buy a car).

2: Because 'would' (and will) can also be used to show if you want to do something or not (volition), we can also use **would have + past participle** to talk about something you wanted to do but didn't. This is very similar to the third conditional, but we don't need an 'if clause'.

- I would have gone to the party, but I was really busy.
  (= I wanted to go to the party, but I didn't because I was busy. If I hadn't been so busy, I would have gone to the party.)

- I would have called you, but I didn't know your number.
  (= I wanted to call you but I didn't know your number, so I didn't call you.)

- A: Nobody volunteered to help us with the fair.
  B: I would have helped you. I didn't know you needed help.
  (= If I had known that you needed help, I would have helped you.)

SIX

LIST OF REGULAR AND IRREGULAR VERBS WITH THEIR FORMS

Regular <u>verbs list</u>:

- *arrange – arranged – arranged*
- *arrive – arrived – arrived*
- *ask – asked – asked*
- *attack – attacked – attacked*
- *bake – baked – baked*
- *behave – behaved – behaved*
- *believe – believed – believed*
- *belong – belonged – belonged*
- *blame – blamed – blamed*
- *borrow – borrowed – borrowed*
- *bother – bothered – bothered*
- *call – called – called*

- *cancel – canceled – canceled*
- *roll – rolled – rolled*

....

Irregular Verbs

There is no formula to predict how <u>an irregular verb</u> will form its past-tense and past-participle forms. There are over 250 irregular verbs in English. Although they do not follow a formula, there are some fairly common irregular forms.

For examples:

- *be – was/ were – been*
- *bear – bore – born (e)*
- *beat – beat – beaten*
- *become – became – become*
- *burst – burst – burst*
- *buy – bought – bought*
- *catch – caught – caught*
- *choose – chose – chosen*
- *cling – clung – clung*
- *come – came – come*
- *cost – cost – cost*
- *creep – crept – crept*

......

SEVEN
VERB TENSES

Verbs come in three tenses: past, present, and future. The past is used to describe things that have already happened (e.g., *earlier in the day, yesterday, last week, three years ago*).

The present tense is used to describe things that are happening right now or things that are continuous. The future tense describes things that have yet to happen (e.g., *later, tomorrow, next week, next year, three years from now*).

Simple Present Tense

The simple present tense is used to express ... universal truths, Narrate past events in the form of a story, Repeated actions, to express situations now.

Structure 1: Subject + Verb 1 + Object.

- I eat dosa every day.

Structure 2: Subject + (Verb 1+s/es/ies) + Object.

- He eats dosa every day.

Simple Present Tense Verbs for He/She/It and Singular Nouns	
Spelling Rules	**Examples**
With most verbs, add s	live - lives sit — sits stay - stays
Ending in consonant + y change y to i and add es	try — tries carry — carries
Ending in s, z, ch, or x add es	miss — misses buzz — buzzes catch — catches fix - fixes
Exceptions	go — goes do - does

Clue words/signal words: Always, often, usually, sometimes, seldom, never. Every day, every week, every year, on Mondays, after school.

Simple Past Tense

Simple past tense is used to express.... completed works, actions, past habits, etc.

Structure: Subject+ Verb2 + Object.

- I ate dosa yesterday.
- Last night, I *read* an entire novel.
- I *taught* English Grammar yesterday.

Clue words/signal words: yesterday, ago, last year, once, etc.

Simple Future Tense

The simple future tense is used to express ...... future actions, to predict future events, to express spontaneous decisions, to express willingness, future facts, plans, or intentions.

Structure: Subject + Shall / Will + Verb1 + Object.

- I shall eat dosa tomorrow.
- He will eat dosa tomorrow.
- I *will read* as much as I can this year.
- I *will teach* English comprehension in the near future.

Clue words/signal words: tomorrow, next week, soon, tonight

Present Continuous Tense

Present continuous tense is used to express ... the actions which are taking place at the time of speaking.

Structure: Subject+ Be form+Verb1 + ing (V4) +Object.

- I am teaching English now.
- We are learning English now.
- Abhi is sleeping now.
- I *am reading* Shakespeare at the moment.
- I *am teaching* Tenses at present.

Clue words/signal words: now, at present, at this point of time, still.

NOTE: We can not use these verbs(stative) in continuous tenses. **Stative verb**: Expressing a state or condition rather than an activity or event see, taste, hear, smell, touch, understand, know, remember, love, like, hate, believe, feel, think, want, continue. etc.

Past Continuous Tense

Past continuous tense is used to express....the continuity of an action at a particular time in the past.

Structure: Subject +Was/Were + Verb 4 + Object.

- I was preparing for a quiz last night.
- You were preparing for a quiz last night.
- Shilpa was preparing for a quiz last night.
- I *was reading* Edgar Allan Poe last night.
- I *was teaching* Verbs an hour ago.

Clue words/signal words: yesterday, last night, at 5 o'clock this morning, at this time yesterday, by that time, while, when.

Future Continuous

Future continuous tense is used to express …… the actions which are expected to be continuous at a particular time in the future.

Structure: Subject + Shall be / Will be + Verb4 + Object.

- I shall be watching a movie tomorrow.
- Abhi will be watching a movie tomorrow.
- They will be watching a movie tomorrow.
- I *will be reading* Nathaniel Hawthorne soon.
- I *will be teaching* literature in some years.

Clue words/signal words: At 10 '0' clock today, at this time tomorrow, by this time next year, by the next month, by 4 '0' clock, by the next year, later.

Present Perfect Tense

a. Present perfect tense is used to express … just completed actions.

Ex: I have just taken my breakfast.

b. Present perfect tense is used to express … A past action when time is not mentioned.

Ex: Venu has completed his degree in 2018. (X)

Venu has completed his degree recently ($\sqrt{}$)

Structure: Subject + Have/Has + Verb3 + Object.

I, We, You, They = have He, She, It = has

- I have gone to the market just now.
- You have gone to market just now.
- Abhi has gone to market just now.
- I *have read* so many books I can't keep count.
- I *have taught* many things so far.

Clue words/signal words: just, already, recently, just now

Past Perfect Tense

The past perfect tense is used to express.... When a sentence has two past actions, we use past perfect to express the first completed action and a simple past for the next one.

Structure: Subject +Had + Verb3 + Object.

- The train had left already when I reached the station.
- I *had read* at least 100 books by the time I was twelve.
- I *had taught* almost entire Grammar to my brother last year.

Clue words/signal words: already + when, before, after, by the time.

Future Perfect Tense

The future perfect tense is used to express ...... the actions which are expected to be completed before or by a particular time in the future.

Structure: Subject + Shall/Will + have + Verb3 + Object.

I, we = shall have you, they, he, she, it = will have

- I shall have completed my work before 11 PM this night.
- Abhi will have gone on a holiday by this time next year.

- I *will have read* at least 500 books by the end of the year.
- I *will have taught* English to almost fifty students by the end of next month.

Clue words/signal words: until, before the end of the day, by the end of the week, by the end of the month, by this time next year, before 10 o'clock this night

Present Perfect Continuous Tense

It is used to express the long-time continuity of action. It means the action which started in the long past and is still continuous.

Structure: Subject + Have/Has been + Verb4 + Object.

I, we, you, they = have been He, she, it = has been

- I have been living in Delhi since 1998.
- Abhi has been repairing the car for 2 hours.
- I *have been reading* since I was four years old.
- I *have been teaching* since morning.

Clue words/signal words: Since (to a point of a time), for (to a period of time), for a long time, for 3 hours, for 10 years, since 2005, since Sunday.

Past Perfect Continuous

Past Perfect Continuous Tense is used to express .... the long-time continuity of an action at a particular time in the past.

Structure: Subject + Had been + Verb4 + Object.

- I had been working in Anantapur for 8 years by the time I transferred.
- Venkat had been studying since 7 o'clock that day morning.

- I *had been reading* for at least a year before my sister learned to read.
- I *had been teaching* when you came home yesterday.

Clue words/signal words:for,since,before,all day
Future Perfect Continuous

Future perfect continuous tense is used .... To express the long-time continuity of an action at a particular time in the future.

Structure: Subject + Shall/Will + have been + Verb 4 + Object.

I, we = shall You, they, he, she, it = will

- I shall have been working in this college for 10 years by 2024.
- My parents will have been traveling for a long time by the time tomorrow.
- I *will have been reading* for at least two hours before dinner tonight.
- I *will have been teaching* by the time you leave.

Clue words/signal words: for, since, before, by the time, all-day

EIGHT

PHRASES TO AGREE OR DISAGREE

How to express agreement or disagreement

1. *Agreeing:*

   - I tend to agree with you.
   - That's a good idea.
   - I'm with you on that point.
   - I'll go along with that.
   - Absolutely! I agree with your point.
   - I totally agree with that idea/proposal.
   - I hold exactly the same view.
   - I couldn't agree more.
   - You're dead right.
   - That's absolutely true.
   - That's just what I was thinking.
   - That's spot on.

- ○ That's exactly my position.
- ○ You've hit the nail on the head!
- ○ That's how I see it too / how I feel too.

2. **Disagreeing**:

- ○ I see things differently.
- ○ I tend to disagree with that idea.
- ○ I agree up to a point. However ...
- ○ You have a point there, but ...
- ○ Sorry, but I think you've missed the point.
- ○ You could be right. However ...
- ○ The idea is worth considering, but ...
- ○ Perhaps a weakness of this is that ...
- ○ Well, I'm not sure of that because ...
- ○ That might be acceptable if ...
- ○ I'm afraid I don't agree / I disagree.
- ○ I strongly / totally disapprove of the plan.
- ○ I'm absolutely against the proposal.

NINE

ASKING FOR OPINIONS

How to ask Someone's opinion?

Do you have any views on ... ?

This page lists useful expressions for the language function of **asking for opinions**.

Elementary

1. Do you think ... ?
2. How do you feel about... ?
3. In your opinion, ... ?
4. Please tell me your opinion on ...
5. What do you think about ... ?
6. What's your opinion on ... ?

Pre-intermediate

1. Do you (also) think that ... ?
2. Do you believe that ... ?
3. Do you have an opinion on ... ?
4. Do you have any opinion on/about ... ?

5. In your experience, ... ?
6. In your honest opinion, ... ?
7. What's your view on ... ?
8. Would you agree that ... ?

Intermediate

1. Can you give me your thoughts on ... ?
2. Do you (dis)approve of ... ?
3. Do you agree with the opinion that ... ?
4. Do you have any views on ... ?
5. Do you share the/my view that ... ?
6. If I asked your opinion about ... , ... ?
7. If I said ... , ... ?
8. I'd like (to hear) your views on ...
9. I'm sure you'd agree that ...
10. What are your feelings about ... ?
11. What are your views on ... ?

Upper-intermediate

1. What do you reckon?
2. Any (initial) thoughts on ... ?
3. Are people right in thinking ... ?
4. Are you in agreement with ... ?
5. Do you have any particular views on ... ?
6. Do you have any thoughts on ... ?
7. From your point of view, ... ?
8. I know this is not your specialist subject, but ...
9. I know you haven't had long to think about this ...
10. I know you haven't had much time to think about this, but ...
11. I'd be (very) interested to hear your views on ...

12. What are your (first) thoughts on … ?
13. What would be your reaction if I said … ?
14. What's your position on … ?
15. Would it be right to say … ?
16. Would you support the view that … ?

Advanced

1. Am I justified in saying … ?
2. Am I right in thinking … ?
3. Any objections to the statement … ?
4. Are you convinced by the argument that … ?
5. Are you of the opinion that … ?
6. Does … tally with your experience?
7. I imagine you will have strong opinions on …
8. I'd guess your view on this is …
9. Is it in fact the case that … ?
10. What reaction do you have to … ?
11. What's your take on … ?
12. Would I be right in assuming that you think … ?
13. Would I be right in saying … ?
14. Would I/it be wrong to say … ?
15. Would it be logical to say … ?
16. Would you have any problems with the statement … ?
17. Would … be a fair summary of your views on … ?
18. Would … be out of the question?
19. You strike me as someone who would hold the opinion that …

TEN
GOOD & BAD NEWS

How to Respond to Good News in English
Professional

- That's great!
- Well done!
- I'm (so/really) glad to hear that!
- Wonderful! Thank you for sharing.
- I'm/we're very happy for you.
- Congratulations.
- That's very good news.

Informal

- Wow! That's awesome!
- Fantastic/great/awesome!
- That's so great!
- I'm thrilled for you!
- I'm so happy for you!
- Congratulations!

- That is good news.
- I can't believe it! That's great!
- Really? Are you serious!?!

Professional & Informal Ways to Give Good News in English

Professional

I'm/we're really pleased to tell you that... I'm pleased to say you got the job.

I'd like to tell you that... I'd like to tell you we accepted your offer.

I'm/we're (really) happy to inform you that... I'm happy to inform you that your application has been approved.

I've/we've got some good news for you... We've got good news for you. Your request to present at the conference was accepted.

Informal

Guess what... Guess what, I got the job!!

I have some amazing/incredible/fantastic/great news for you... I have some amazing news! I was accepted to the university.

Can you believe it... Can you believe it? She passed the exam!

I'm so excited to tell you that... I'm excited to tell you that we're getting married!

Informal Ways to Respond to Bad News in English

These responses are best for close friends, family members, and colleagues when the news is bad or disappointing but not terrible.

For example:

- canceling dinner plans
- working overtime on the weekend

- losing your cell phone
- spilling ketchup on your new shirt
- getting a cold

Common Responses:

- Oh no, that stinks!
- What a bummer.
- Oh, I'm sorry.
- That's awful.
- Sorry, that's rough/awful/disappointing.
- Hope you feel better. (Used when someone isn't feeling well or is getting sick.)

Formal Ways to Respond to Bad News in English

These responses are best for work colleagues or acquaintances or when the news is truly bad.

For example:

- Losing a job
- Losing a pet
- Getting into a car accident
- Losing a big client

Common Expressions:

- I'm so sorry to hear that!
- What awful news! I'm sorry.
- I'm sorry to hear such terrible news.
- I'm very sorry – that must be awful/frustrating/scary/difficult.
- If there's anything I can do, just let me know.

- I really don't know what to say, I can't believe it. I'm very sorry.

Ways to Respond to Very Sad or Shocking News in English

When friends, colleagues, family members share news of grief such as the death of someone or divorce, these expressions are the most appropriate.

Common Expressions:

- I'm terribly sorry to hear that.
- How terrible/sad/awful – I'm so sorry.
- I'm sorry. Is there anything I can do to help?
- I'm very sorry about your loss. (Used to express sympathy for news of a death.)
- Please accept my sincerest condolences/sympathies. (Used to express sympathy for news of a death.)
- If you need anything, I'm here for you.
- My heart hurts for you. I'm very sorry.

ELEVEN

CONFUSED WORDS IN ENGLISH

Top 30 Commonly Confused Words in English

Everyone knows the problem with spell-check: your word might be spelled right, but it may be the wrong word. English is full of confusing words that sound alike but are spelled differently. It's also full of words that share similar (but not identical) meanings that are easy to misuse. Below are some of the most commonly confused and misused words.

1. **Advice/Advise** *Advice* is a noun: Chester gave Posey good advice. *Advise* is a verb: Chester advised Posey to avoid the questionable chicken salad.

2. **Affect/Effect** *Affect* is usually a verb: Chester's humming affected Posey's ability to concentrate. *Effect* is usually a noun: Chester was sorry for the effect his humming had. If you find yourself stumped about which one to use in a

sentence, try substituting the word "alter" or "result." If "alter" fits (Chester's humming altered Posey's ability to concentrate), use *affect*. If "result" fits (Chester was sorry for the result his humming had), use *effect*.

3. **Among/Amongst***Among* is the preferred and most common variant of this word in American English. *Amongst* is more common in British English. Neither version is wrong, but *amongst* may seem fussy to American readers.

4. **Among/Between***Among* expresses a collective or loose relationship of several items: Chester found a letter hidden among the papers on the desk. *Between* expresses the relationship of one thing to another thing or to many other things: Posey spent all day carrying messages between Chester and the other students. The idea that *between* can be used only when talking about two things is a myth—it's perfectly correct to use *between* if you are talking about multiple binary relationships.

5. **Assure/Ensure/Insure***Assure* means to tell someone that something will definitely happen or is definitely true: Posey assured Chester that no one would cheat at Bingo. *Ensure* means to guarantee or make sure of something: Posey took steps to ensure that no one cheated at Bingo. *Insure* means to take out an insurance policy: Posey was glad the Bingo hall was insured against damage caused by rowdy Bingo players.

6. **Breath/Breathe***Breath* is a noun; it's the air that goes in and out of your lungs: Chester held his breath while Posey skateboarded down the stairs. *Breathe* is a verb; it means to exhale or inhale: After Posey's spectacular landing, Chester had to remind himself to breathe again.

7. **Capital/Capitol***Capital* has several meanings. It can refer to an uppercase letter, money, or a city where a

seat of government is located: Chester visited Brasília, the capital of Brazil. *Capitol* means the building where a legislature meets: Posey visited the cafe in the basement of the capitol after watching a bill become a law.

8. **Complement/Compliment** A *complement* is something that completes something else. It's often used to describe things that go well together: Chester's lime green boots were a perfect complement to his jacket. A *compliment* is a nice thing to say: Posey received many compliments on her purple fedora.

9. **Disinterested/Uninterested** *Disinterested* means impartial: A panel of disinterested judges who had never met the contestants before judged the singing contest. *Uninterested* means bored or not wanting to be involved with something: Posey was uninterested in attending Chester's singing class.

10. **Defence/Defense** *Defense* is standard in American English. *Defence* is found mainly in British English.

11. **Emigrate/Immigrate** *Emigrate* means to move away from a city or country to live somewhere else: Chester's grandfather emigrated from Canada sixty years ago. *Immigrate* means to move into a country from somewhere else: Posey's sister immigrated to Ireland in 2004.

12. **E.g./I.e.** These two Latin abbreviations are often mixed up, but *e.g.* means "for example," while *i.e.* means "that is."

13. **Empathy/Sympathy** *Empathy* is the ability to understand another person's perspective or feelings. *Sympathy* is a feeling of sorrow for someone else's suffering. A *sympathizer* is someone who agrees with a particular ideal or cause.

14. **Farther/Further** *Farther* refers to physical distance: Posey can run farther than Chester. *Further* refers to metaphorical distance: Chester is further away from finishing his project than Posey is.

15. **Flaunt/Flout** *Flaunt* means to show off: Chester flaunted his stylish new outfit. *Flout* means to defy, especially in a way that shows scorn: Posey flouted the business-casual dress code by wearing a tiara and flip-flops.

16. **Gaff/Gaffe** A *gaff* is a type of spear or hook with a long handle: Chester completed his sailor costume with a gaff borrowed from his uncle's fishing boat. A *gaffe* is a faux pas or social misstep: Posey made a gaffe when she accidentally called Chester by the wrong name.

17. **Gray/Grey** *Gray* is the standard American English spelling. *Grey* is the standard British English spelling.

18. **Historic/Historical** *Historic* means famous, important, and influential: Chester visited the beach in Kitty Hawk where the Wright brothers made their historic first airplane flight. *Historical* means related to history: Posey donned a historical bonnet for the renaissance fair.

19. **Imply/Infer** *Imply* means to hint at something without saying it directly: Chester implied that Posey was in trouble, but he wouldn't tell her why. *Infer* means to deduce something that hasn't been stated directly: Posey inferred that Chester was nervous about something from the way he kept looking over his shoulder.

20. **It's/Its** *It's* is a contraction of "it is": Posey needs to pack for her trip because it's only two days away. *Its* is a possessive pronoun that means "belonging to it": Chester is obsessed with both the book and its author.

21. **Lay/Lie** *To lay* means to put or to place. One way to remember this is that there is an a in both *to lay* and *to place*: Posey will lay out her outfit before she goes to bed.

To lie means to recline. One way to remember this is that there is an e in both *to lie* and *to recline*: Chester will lie down for a nap. Be careful, though. The past tense of *to lay* is *laid*: Posey laid out her outfit. The past tense of *to lie* is *lay*: Chester lay down for a nap over an hour ago.

22. **Lead/Led***Lead*, when it rhymes with "bed," refers to a type of metal: Posey wore a lead apron while the dentist X-rayed her teeth. *Led* is the past tense of the verb *to lead*, which means to guide or to be first: Chester led the way.

23. **Learned/Learnt***Learned* is standard in American English. *Learnt* is standard in British English.

24. **Loose/Lose***Loose* is usually an adjective: Posey discovered that the cows were loose. *Lose* is always a verb. It means to misplace something or to be un-victorious in a game or contest: Chester was careful not to lose his ticket.

25. **Principal/Principle***Principal* can be a noun or adjective. As a noun, it refers to the person in charge of a school or organization: Posey was called into the principal's office. As an adjective, it means most important: The principal reason for this meeting is to brainstorm ideas for the theme of Chester's birthday party. A *principle* (always a noun) is a firmly held belief or ideal: Posey doesn't like surprise parties as a matter of principle.

26. **Inquiry/Enquiry***Inquiry* and *enquiry* both mean "a request for information." *Inquiry* is the standard American English spelling. *Enquiry* is the British spelling.

27. **Stationary/Stationery***Stationary* means unmoving: The revolving door remained stationary because Posey was pushing on it the wrong way. *Stationery* refers to letter writing materials and especially to high-quality paper: Chester printed his résumé on his best stationery.

28. **Than/Then***Than* is used for comparisons: Posey runs faster than Chester. *Then* is used to indicate time or sequence: Posey took off running, and then Chester came along and finished her breakfast.

29. **Their/There/They're***Their* is the possessive form of "they": Chester and Posey took their time. *There* indicates a place: It took them an hour to get there. *They're* is a contraction of "they are": Are Chester and Posey coming? They're almost here.

30. **To/Too***To* is a preposition that can indicate direction: Posey walked to school. She said hello to Chester when she saw him. *To* is also used in the infinitive form of verbs: Chester waited until the last minute to do his homework. *Too* is used as an intensifier, and also means "also": Posey waited too long to do her homework, too.

31. **Toward/Towards***Toward* is standard in American English. *Towards* is standard in British English.

32. **Who's/Whose***Who's* is a contraction of "who is": Who's calling Chester at this hour? *Whose* is a possessive pronoun that means "belonging to [someone]": Chester, whose phone hadn't stopped ringing all morning, barely ate anything for breakfast.

TWELVE
PHRASAL VERBS

USEFUL PHRASAL VERBS WITH UP

1. **Blow up** (explode): The car blew up after it crashed into the wall.
2. **Bring up** (Look after a child until it grows up, usually children): They brought up their children to be responsible adults.
3. **Bring up** (Introduce or mention a subject): Bring it up at the meeting!
4. **Build up** (Make a business bigger, to develop contacts or a presence): We have built up the business over the years and it now employs over 2000 people."
5. **Build up** (Increase over time): It's important to build up your muscle strength over time.
6. **Burn up** (Destroy something): The spacecraft burned up as it entered the earth's atmosphere.
7. **Burn up** (Make somebody very angry): The way he treats me really burns me up.
8. **Call up** (Telephone): I'm going to call up and cancel my subscription.

9. **Call up** (Bring back to your mind): The smell of the sea called up memories of her childhood.
10. **Catch up** (Reach somebody who's in front of you): Go on ahead. I'll catch up with you.
11. **Catch up** (To reach the same level or standard as somebody who was better or more advanced): After missing a term through illness he had to work hard to catch up with the others.
12. **Catch up** (To finish off pending work): I need to catch up with all my work over the weekend.
13. **Check up** (To make sure that somebody is doing what they should be doing): My parents are always checking up on me.
14. **Check up** (Obtain information about somebody or something to find out if something is true or correct): I need to check up on a few things before I can decide.
15. **Cheer up** (To make someone happier): Can you cheer Tim up?
16. **Chop up** (Cut into small pieces): Can you chop up some carrots for me?
17. **Come up** (Happen unexpectedly): I'm afraid I can't make the meeting tomorrow. Something has come up."
18. **Divide up** (Distribute): We can divide up the commission among the sales staff.
19. **Divide up** (Force up the prices or costs): The uncertainty in the markets is dividing up labour costs.
20. **Do up** (Fasten up): Do you know how to do up your seat belt?
21. **Do up** (Arrange hair so that it's tied or fastened close): We should do up our hair before cooking any meal.
22. **Do up** (To repair and decorate a house, etc.): He makes money by buying old houses and doing them up.

23. **Dress up** (To wear a fancy dress, a costume to disguise yourself): He dressed up as a pirate, for the party.
24. **Dress up** (Put on clothes): There's no need to dress up—come as you are.
25. **Eat up** (To eat all the food that you've been given): If you eat up all your vegetables, you can have dessert.
26. **End up** (Eventually do/decide): We ended up going to the theatre instead of the gallery.
27. **Get up** (Get out of bed): I got up early this morning and went for a walk.
28. **Give up** (abandoning to do something/to stop doing something): Time to give up!
29. **Go up** (To increase): The price of petrol went up in March.
30. **Grow up** (To become an adult): I'm 18, I'm a grown-up now!
31. **Heat up** (To make it hotter): I'll heat the soup up for lunch.
32. **Hurry up** (To rush): You guys should hurry up if you don't want to miss the train.
33. **Lookup** (Find someone, search for something): Did you look up the telephone number of the restaurant?
34. **Makeup** (Invent, lie about something): Don't believe everything she tells you. She likes making up stories.
35. **Make-up** (Compensate): I still need more money to make up for the losses.
36. **Meet up** (Make an arrangement to meet): What time should we meet up on Wednesday?
37. **Open up** (Start to talk freely about something): She hates to open up and discuss her feelings.
38. **Pass up** (To not take an opportunity): We can't pass up this chance of increasing productivity.

39. **Pass on** (To hand over something): I passed on my assignments to my friend for completion. / We should always try to pass on our culture to our upcoming generation.

40. **Pick up** (To improve over time): My health has picked up over the past few days.

41. **Put up** (To raise): We'll have to put our prices up to compete with the market.

42. **Put up** (To arrange/conduct): They are going to put up a grand show tomorrow.

43. **Set up** (Arrange): I'll help you set up for the party as soon as I get home.

44. **Show up** (Arrive/Appear): You can rely on Jim to show up on time.

45. **Show off** (To Brag/Boast about something): In metro cities, people always like to show off.

46. **Speak up** (To speak with a stronger voice): You need to speak up for people to understand you.

47. **Speed up** (To go faster in a vehicle): He quickly sped up to sixty miles an hour.

48. **Stand up** (To be on your feet): There were no seats left so I had to stand up.

49. **Startup** (to start something new): They've started up a new division in Southern Europe.

50. **Take up** (Start): Have you taken up any new hobbies lately?

51. **Turn up**(To raise the volume): I like to turn the stereo up when nobody is home.

52. **Warm-up** (To make it hotter): I'll warm this soup up for lunch.

53. **Write up** (Write a report for minutes): It'll take him at least a week to write up his findings.

54. **Back up** (Cause to move backward): You can back up another two feet or so.
55. **Back up** (Support or help someone): The rebels backed up their demands with threats.
56. **Draw up** (Prepare a written document): They agreed to draw up a formal agreement.
57. **Draw up** (If a vehicle draws up, it arrives and stops): The cab drew up outside the house.
58. **Fix up** (Repair): They fixed up the house before they moved in.

THIRTEEN

PHRASES FOR ASKING INFORMATION

Popular Expressions for Asking for Information

- I'm looking for...
- I'd <u>like</u> to know...
- Do you know...?
- Could you tell me...?
- Can you tell me...?
- Do you have any idea...?
- I don't suppose you know...?
- I'm calling to find out...
- I wonder if someone could tell me...?
- Do you happen to know...?
- Have you got an idea of...?
- Don't suppose you (would) know...?
- Can I have ... please?

- Is this the right way for ...? (<u>Asking for and Giving Directions</u>)
- Would you mind...?
- Could anyone tell me...?
- I'm interested in...
- I wonder if you could tell me...?
- I was wondering...

FOURTEEN

Phrases for Talking about Future Plans

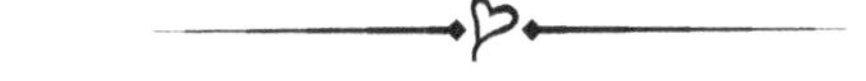

English Phrases for Talking About Future Plans

1. I'm going to...
2. I'm planning to...
3. I hope to...
4. I'd like to...
5. I might... / I may...
6. I'm thinking about...

1. LOSE WEIGHT
Other ways to say it / related goals:

- lose 10 pounds
- get back into shape

- get in better shape
- work out more
  (*work out = exercise*)
- eat healthier / eat less / eat more fruits and vegetables
- cut down on junk food
  (*junk food = unhealthy food*)

2. GET ORGANIZED
Other ways to say it / related goals:

- manage my time better
- stop procrastinating / stop putting things off
  (*procrastinating / putting things off = delaying your tasks and responsibilities = postponing*)
- be more punctual
  (*punctual = arrive on time for meetings, appointments, and social commitments*)
- stick to my schedule
  (*stick to = follow, accompany closely*)
- have a better work-life balance

3. SPEND LESS, SAVE MORE
Other ways to say it / related goals:

- save up for __________ (a new car, a house, a trip)
- get out of debt / pay off debt
  (*debt = money you owe and need to pay back*)
- pay off my student loans / pay off my mortgage
  (*student loans = money you borrowed to pay for education*)
  (*mortgage = money you borrowed to pay for a house*)
- make a budget and stick to it
  (*budget = specific plan for spending money in various areas*)

4. QUIT SMOKING / DRINKING
Other ways to say it / related goals:

- kick the smoking habit / habit of smoking
  (*kick = stop doing, eliminate*)
- drink in moderation
  (*in moderation = a reasonable amount, not too much*)
- lay off the alcohol
  (*lay off = stop using/consuming so much*)

5. SPEND MORE TIME WITH FAMILY
Other ways to say it / related goals:

- improve my marriage
- play with my kids more
- reconnect with old friends
  (*reconnect = contact again after some time without contact*)
- show my family how much I love them
- be a better husband/wife/mother/father

Phrases For Making Resolutions:
I'M GOING TO... / I'M NOT GOING TO...
Use these phrases to state promises and intentions. Add the word "definitely" for extra emphasis.

- This year, **I'm definitely going to** learn a new language.
- From now on, **I'm not going to** eat at McDonald's.

I'M DETERMINED TO... / I'M DETERMINED NOT TO...
These phrases express your firm emotional commitment to your goals.

- **I'm determined to** eat healthier in 2016.

- **I'm determined not to** lose my temper with my kids.
  "lose your temper" means to explode in anger

I'M PLANNING TO + (BASE FORM)
I'M PLANNING ON + (-ING FORM)
This phrase is for plans that are more definite; you've already taken steps to make them happen.

- **I'm planning to travel** to Hawaii this September.
- **We're planning on buying** a house within the next 12 months.

I HOPE TO... / I'D LIKE TO...
Use these phrases for things you want, but there's less certainty that they will happen.

- **I hope to** get into graduate school this year.
- **I'd like to** find a better-paying job as soon as possible.

I MIGHT... / I'M THINKING ABOUT...
Use these when YOU'RE not completely certain; you are only considering the idea.

- **I might** get a dog, although I'm not sure if my apartment's big enough for a pet.
- **I'm thinking about** having another child this year.

Phrases For Expressing Excitement/Anticipation
Use these phrases when something will DEFINITELY happen in the future, and you are excited about it.

- **I'm looking forward to + ING**
  I'm looking forward to starting guitar lessons.

I'm really looking forward to visiting my cousins in June – I haven't seen them in five years!

- **I can't wait to + base form / I can't wait for + noun**
  I can't wait to see the new Star Wars movie.
  I can't wait for summer vacation!
- **I'm counting down the days until...**
  I'm counting down the days until the end of the semester.
- Informal: **I'm psyched/pumped to + verb / about + noun**
  I'm psyched about the opportunity to go to China.
  I'm pumped to start my new job in February.

Future Perfect

Finally, you can use the future perfect to talk about what you hope to accomplish before the year ends:

- By the end of the year, **I will have run** a marathon.
- By the end of the year, **I will have improved** my English.
- By the end of the year, **I will have saved up** $10,000.
- By the end of the year, **I will have gotten** a promotion.

The structure is **will + have + past participle.**

FIFTEEN

WORDS TO SAY INSTEAD OF VERY

Very angry-*Furious*
Very beautiful-*Gorgeous*
Very big-*Massive*
Very boring-*Dull*
Very noisy-*Deafening*
Very poor-*Destitute*
Very cheap- *Stingy*
Very clean-*Spotless*
Very short (information)-*Brief*
Very difficult-*Arduous*
Very dry-*Arid*
Very quick-*Rapid*
Very bad-*Awful*
Very smart/clever-*Intelligent*
Very sad-*Sorrowful*
Very upset-*Distraught*
Very cold-*Freezing*
Very strong-*Forceful*
Very huge-*Colossal*

Very calm-*Serene*
Very ugly-*Hideous*
Very small-*Petite*
Very funny-*Hilarious*
Very quiet-*Hushed*
Very rich-*Wealthy*
Very costly-*Expensive*
Very dirty-*Filthy*
Very tall-*Towering*
Very easy-*Effortless*
Very wet-*Soaked*
Very slow-*Sluggish*
Very good-*Excellent*
Very stupid-*Idiotic*
Very happy-*Ecstatic*
Very exciting-*Exhilarating*
Very warm-*Hot*
Very weak-*Frail*
Very little-*Tiny*
Very fancy-*Lavish*
Very fat-*Obese*
Very friendly-*Amiable*
Very glad-*Overjoyed*
Very great-*Terrific*
Very heavy-*Leaden*
Very hungry/starving-*Famished*
Very large-*Huge*
Very hurt-*Battered*
Very lazy-*Indolent*
Very long-*Extensive*
Very loose-*Slack*
Very accurate-*Exact*
Very afraid-*Fearful*

Very cute/lovely-*Adorable*
Very dull/ Tiresome-*Tedious*
Very eager/sharp-*Keen*
Very evil-*Wicked*
Very fast-*Quick*
Very fierce-*Ferocious*
Very lively-*Jolly*
Very mean-*Cruel*
Very messy-*Slovenly*
Very nice-*Kind*
Very often-*Frequent(ly)*
Very old-*Ancient*
Very open/clear-*Transparent*
Very pale-*Ashen*
Very perfect-*Flawless*
Very powerful-*Compelling*
Very pretty-*Beautiful*
Very rainy-*Pouring*
Very scared-*Petrified*
Very scary-*Horrifying*
Very serious-*Grave*
Very shiny-*Gleaming*
Very shy-*Timid*
Very simple-*Basic*

SIXTEEN

FUNCTIONAL LANGUAGE

Functional language is a language that we use to perform various "functions" such as giving advice or apologizing. Functional language typically uses fixed expressions for each function–for example "if I were you" or "my suggestion is" in giving advice, and "it was my fault" or "please forgive me" in apologizing.

- Giving Advice
  if I were you, my suggestion is...

- Making Requests
  can I, may I ask, I'd like to request...

- Apologizing
  it was my fault, please forgive me..

- Giving Bad News
  I'm sorry to say, I tried my best but...

- Agreeing
  you're right, I feel the same way...

- Disagreeing
  I don't really agree, but what about...

- Disagreeing Strongly
  absolutely not, rubbish! I can't accept it...

- Offering
  shall I, can I give you a hand...

- Asking for Opinions
  in your opinion, what's your view on...

- Giving Opinions
  I feel that I could be wrong but...

We're especially going to focus on functional language that you can use in conversation or when you have to speak for a long time about a complicated topic, as you might for an English-speaking exam, or a school or work presentation.

We'll start by learning more about functional language. Then, we'll discuss how we use functional language in English for:

- Putting information or events in order
- Clarifying information
- Summarizing information
- Focusing on specific details
- Showing an exception

We use the term functional language to talk about the specific words, phrases, and expressions that we use in a particular interaction.

It's different from learning straightforward grammar or vocabulary. **The goal of functional language is to help you learn specific phrases and expressions that you can use in situations** at work, in travel, or when meeting new people.

That doesn't mean that grammar and vocabulary aren't also important. But usually, functional language takes the specific student's needs into account.

To figure out what functional language you might need to learn, it helps to ask:

- What specific things do I need to do or accomplish with English?
- What is my lifestyle like?
- What am I interested in?
- What do I like to talk about?
- What kinds of words, phrases, or expressions will help me thrive in a situation that I'm likely to encounter in the future?

So, with that in mind, let's take a look at some different functional expressions you can use to express yourself and your ideas with confidence.

Putting information or events in order

We use certain phrases and expressions to put events in order of sequence and importance. So, for example, if you need to describe how something works in steps, you can use expressions to show how the steps work in a sequence.

But, if you're expressing your opinion or views about something, you might want to express your main ideas in order of importance instead.

You might have learned expressions like *firstly, secondly, lastly,* or *and then*, but you might not know an expression to discuss things that are related to your main idea or how to explain things in more detail.

Expressions to put information in order of sequence

Here are some expressions that you can use to talk about a process or sequence of steps. Those will be helpful when you need to talk about how to make something or how to make something work:

- *You'll start by/with...*
- *The next thing you'll do is...*
- *After that, you will...*
- *Last, but not least,...*

Here's an example of how we can use these expressions to describe a simple process:

We'll start by *making sure the machine is in the right setting.*

The next thing we'll do is *insert the paper into the machine.*
After that, we'll *hit the "print" button.*

Last but not least, *we'll wait for all the pages to print properly.*

Expressions to put information in order of importance

Sometimes, English learners can get confused between how to describe something in a sequence versus in the order of importance.

Whether you're writing an essay or giving a presentation, it's important to follow some logical steps to make sure that your audience or reader is following you. So, you can use expressions such as:

- *The first point I want to make...*

- *The first issue I want to discuss...*
- *Now let's talk about...*
- *Moving on, I want to explore...*
- *Then let's focus on...*
- *Ultimately...*

Here are some ways you might use these expressions:

- **The first point I want to make** is that education is not accessible to everyone.

- **The first issue I would like to discuss** is our problem with media consumption.

- **Now let's talk about** the fact that gas prices are rising.

- **Moving on, I want to explore** the ways in which we can eliminate waste.

- **Then, let's focus on** how we can implement these policies right away.

- **Ultimately,** it's going to take a lot of work to make these changes, but it's possible.

Did you notice how I used different verbs in the expressions: *make, discuss, talk about, explore,* etc.?

Especially in writing, it's a good idea to use a variety of verbs and structures in your functional language so that your English doesn't feel so repetitive.

Expressions for related details

When it comes to a detailed argument, we also use these English expressions to give supporting details that strengthen our main ideas.

Here are some examples:

- *I should also mention that...*
- *It's also worth considering that...*
- *You should also note...*
- *It's also important to take into account that...*

And we might use them in this way:

- **I should also mention that** *fruits and vegetables are way more expensive than fast food.*
- **It's also worth considering that** *not everyone in this community approves of the construction.*
- **You should also note** *that most people get their news from social media.*
- **It's also important to take into account that** *some countries don't pay teachers enough.*

Clarifying information

Sometimes we need to state or write things in a different or even simpler way in English to make sure that our readers or listeners don't get lost in the details or in a complex argument.

So, that's why it's important to have expressions that can help you clarify information. The great thing about these expressions is that they also help you create more variety in your writing or speaking style, which engages people even more.

Here are a few common examples:

- *What I mean is...*
- *What I'm trying to say is that...*

- *To put it another way...*
- *In simpler terms...*

And here's how we might use them:

- **What I mean is** *that the economy won't benefit from this decision.*
- **What I'm trying to say is that** *people didn't like her writing.*
- **To put it another way,** *people just need to work harder.*
- **In simpler terms,** *if we don't buy their products, they won't be able to do bad things.*

Summarizing information

When we come to the end of one main idea or of a series of arguments, we need to summarize the information that we discussed and the points that we made. This is especially necessary for anyone who wants to write a well-constructed English essay.

But they're not just helpful for writing. They're also helpful for speaking, too, especially if you're discussing something important with someone or if you're defending your unpopular opinion about something.

A summarizing or concluding expression shows your reader or listener that you've come to the end of your argument, and it allows them another chance to process everything you've said or written.

So, here are some expressions that we can use at the end of the main idea or in the conclusion of our argument.

- *All things considered...*
- *With all this in mind...*
- *All this is to say that...*

- *Overall...*

And here are some examples of how we might use them:

- **All things considered,** *I don't think we should consider obesity a public health issue.*
- **With all this in mind,** *students should be allowed to decide if they want a university education.*
- **All this is to say that** *we should try to reduce the stigma around mental health.*
- **Overall,** *I think the benefits of electric cars for the environment outweigh the disadvantages.*

Focusing on specific details

I mentioned some expressions you can use for giving details that are related to your main point earlier, but we also have English expressions that we can use to focus on a specific point we want to make. We can use these expressions when we want to shift our focus from one point to another.

And here are some phrases we can use to do just that!

- *When it comes to...*
- *In terms of...*
- *If we're talking about...*
- *Taking a closer look at...*

Here are some ways that we can use these expressions:

- **When it comes to** *modern-day space travel, Elon Musk claims to have the answers.*
- **In terms of** *downsizing, I think it's better to keep as many employees as we can.*

- ***If we're talking about*** *online dating, some people feel that it's a strange way to meet people.*
- ***Taking a closer lookat*** *the problem, you'll find that it's a complex situation.*

Looking at something a different way

There are times when we want to ask our reader or listener to consider an issue or point from another perspective. This can also help to clarify your argument and show that there are other ways to approach an issue.

For example:

- *Looking at this in another way...*
- *From this angle...*
- *If we think about it a different way...*
- *Taking another look at this issue...*

And we might use these expressions like this:

- ***Looking at this another way,*** *you'll find that the new construction doesn't benefit the local economy.*
- ***From this angle,*** *it's easier to understand why people are so upset about this new policy.*
- ***If we think about it a different way,*** *his argument against smartphones makes sense.*
- ***Taking another look at this issue,*** *our initial problems don't make as much sense.*

Showing an exception

If you've ever had to write an essay for an English exam, you know that sometimes you are asked to consider both sides of an argument. And it's a good thing to do!

It helps make your argument stronger when you can "play devil's advocate," that is, to defend a perspective that goes against your own.

Here are some expressions we can use to show exceptions to a certain argument or way of seeing something:

- *Still...*
- *Regardless of the fact that...*
- *I admit that...*
- *While it's true that...*

Keep in mind, we often use these expressions to connect two clauses or sentences that contrast each other.

So, we often use them in this way:

- *Some people believe that not all speech should be free.* **Still,** *it's hard to decide what speech shouldn't be free.*
- **Regardless of the fact that** *the new construction will cause a lot of traffic, I think it's going to benefit our local economy.*
- **I admit that** *driverless cars seem like an exciting idea, but they're actually more dangerous than you might expect.*
- **While it's true that** *elementary students benefit from homework in some ways, it still prevents them from the free time they might spend with their families.*

How can I use more functional language in my everyday English practice?

My first piece of advice here is to take it slowly. Don't try to learn a long list of functional phrases and expressions all at once. That will only overwhelm and discourage you.

Instead, take five to seven new phrases at a time, and focus on learning and practicing with those for a couple of weeks. Then move on to a new set of phrases.

So, what should you do to practice? Think about the ways you learn best. If you're a visual learner, write the phrases out on cards or print them out and put the paper in a place you will see them all the time. Every time you look at them, try to use at least one of them in a sentence.

Then, of course, use them in speech and writing! Record yourself speaking with some functional phrases for a few minutes a day. Challenge yourself to write at least two sentences with these phrases every day. Keeping your practice small is great, especially if it will encourage you to do it every day in the form of role play.

How do you write a role play dialogue?

How to Use Role Play

1. Step 1: Identify the Situation. To start the process, gather people together, introduce the problem, and encourage an open discussion to uncover all of the relevant issues. ...

2. Step 2: Add Details. ...
3. Step 3: Assign Roles. ...
4. Step 4: Act Out the Scenario. ...
5. Step 5: Discuss What You Have Learned.

How do you make Roleplay interesting?

Tips To Make Your Role Play Better

1. Get To Know Your Character Before You Roleplay. ...
2. Read Your Partner's Reply Well And When You're Done, Read It Again. ...
3. Write Your Replies To The Length Of Your Partner's. ...
4. Make Clear Separations Between Dialogue And Action. ...
5. Shake Up Your Storyline With Conflict.

Do you want to know the secret to becoming one of the best Roleplayers out there? Imagination. Oh, so you have imagination, do you? Then why are you still looking for RP?

Well, keep reading. Here are some tips and tricks to help you on your Roleplay journey, and to become an RPer *everyone* will want to write with.

1. Get To Know Your Character Before You Roleplay

2. Read Your Partner's Reply Well And When You're Done, Read It Again

Roleplay is about responding to what your partner is saying. If you're not willing to carefully read your partner's reply, go ahead and write a solo story and rethink your plans for RP.

3. Write Your Replies To The Length Of Your Partner's

There's nothing more frustrating than working hard on a detailed reply and waiting for your partner's response, only to receive a line or two back. RP writing takes time. And great RP takes a lot of time. The old saying, you reap what you sow is so true. Don't be surprised when you drive your partner away by not giving back replies as good as you're getting.

4. Make Clear Separations Between Dialogue And Action

5. Shake Up Your Storyline With Conflict

Keeping a strong storyline going is not an easy thing to do. Real-life often gets in the way of finishing, but boredom also plays a role in extinguishing our fire to keep going. The same old stuff, day after day, reply after reply, can get incredibly dull. But having a storyline filled with dramatic highs and lows will not only make your RP more interesting, but it'll also help you develop your character through those rocky times.

Conflict is what brings dimension to our characters. It's in finding solutions to problems or fighting their way through the storm that brings out their best or worst qualities. There are so many cookie-cutter RP characters out there. We call these characters Mary Sues and Gary Stus because they're just so perfect.

What kind of conflict can you plunge your characters into that will make them work the hardest and prove they're truly unique?

6. There's More To Roleplay Than Shipping

If you're coming into RP focused on shipping your character, this will be a glaring red light to other Roleplayers. Desperation to ship is easy to spot, and many are wary of this call to romance.

Even if you're already in a ship with your partner, if all you ever do is romance and sexy stuff, it's likely to get dull over time. Yes, even love, and sex gets boring in RP land. But if you bring in dramatic storylines like unfaithfulness or addiction, you might soon look forward to writing the makeup love after the battle.

7. Before You Send Your Reply: Read, Edit, Then Read It Out Loud

Every writer makes mistakes, but every great writer knows the importance of editing. As Roleplayers, sending your replies back and forth is part of the fun. But don't send your response back so quickly that you haven't read it over a few times first. Too many mistakes make you look sloppy and not serious about your Roleplaying.

And here's the secret sauce every great writer knows: READ YOUR REPLY OUT LOUD. How many times have you looked back at what you've written and cringed because of a spelling mistake? It's even more frustrating when you post up a mistake and you know you've read your reply over carefully. Well, that happens to all of us.

The best strategy is to give yourself a break between writing and editing so you come back to it with fresh eyes. But if you can't do that, reading your reply out loud engages a different part of your brain to catch those nit-picky mistakes. You'll soon realize you dropped a word or substituted "I" instead of "a" in your sentence.

There are also free services available to help you catch common errors before you send that reply. Grammarly.com is one of those services that can be added as an extension to your internet browser. They even have their own keyboard that will edit your texts on the fly. I religiously use the keyboard app on my phone to double-check for spelling mistakes before I post any reply to my partner.

8. Roleplay Does Not Equal Real Life

Remember, everyone has a life outside of this RP world we love, and real-life always comes first. Have patience for your partner, but also have common sense about your RP relationship. You should not be expected to be actively RPing all the time, and neither should your partner. There is a happy middle ground.

Communicate with each other before you start RPing. Talk about when you expect to send your replies, and when you can't. Make sure to let your partner know, so they're not left wondering. The partners you'll want to keep are those who have patience. But make sure to be equally patient back.

9. Let Your Character Be Miserable, But Avoid Bringing Your Real-Life Misery Into Your RP World

Misery loves company, and that may be true. But chances are, you'll have a harder time finding a writing partner if you're carrying your real-life misery into your account. If you're whining and moaning ur partner might not be sticking around for very long.

For most people, RP writing is a form of escape from their real lives. Their character is near and dear to them, but so is their time. When you become your character, leave your real-life problems and baggage at the RP door. Escape into your storyline with your partner.

10. HAVE FUN!

You're spending your time weaving with your partner and becoming someone else for a little while.

There really are no magic tricks to becoming a great Roleplayer. But by using these simple tips, you'll find your Roleplay to be something you and your partner will want to keep writing for as long as your muse flows.

Making Requests

I was wondering if it would be possible to.......

Is there any chance that I could.......

Would it be alright if I........

I believe I'm entitled to/I deserve...... (a pay rise/a day off)

Giving Reasons

You see the thing is...............

The problem is that.............

Accepting Requests

Ok, I don't see why not.

Of course.

No problem at all

Adding Conditions

As long as/provided that/on condition that you........

Rejecting Requests

I'm afraid that's just not possible at the moment.

That's out of the question.

I'm afraid I have to turn your request down.

Role plays

A:

You are an employee in a company. Next weekend your best friend is having his/her You have to ask your boss for the Monday and Tuesday after off work. Your boss will probably reject the request if he/she knows you are going to a stag/hen party.

B:

You are the boss of the company. An employee comes to ask you something. This particular employee has seemed distracted recently and keeps forgetting important things.

A:

You are and salesperson in a company. You are very stressed and you need a rest, you have decided that you want to take a sabbatical to go and volunteer in an elephant sanctuary in Africa for a year. You need to speak to the boss. You are very hard-working and the company is doing very well because of your hard work.

B:

You are the boss of a company. One of your employees comes to ask you something. You have heard a rumour that this employee wants to take a sabbatical. He/she is your best salesperson and the company really needs him/her. You can offer him/her a pay rise, a promotion and a 1 month holiday.

A:

You are a strict parent. Your son/daughter comes to you with a request about the weekend.

B:

You are a teenager. Your best friend is having a massive party at his/her house this weekend because his/her parents are away, the boy/girl of your dreams is also going to be there. You need to get your parent's permission to go but they are very strict and will not give you permission if they know it's going to be a crazy party.

A:

You are a teacher. Your best student comes to you with a request.

B:

You are a student. You are very intelligent and you work very hard. You want to be a journalist. You have been offered a part-time job in a national newspaper. If you take the job you will have to work from 9 AM-12 AM on Mondays Wednesdays and Fridays but you have classes on these days. Speak to your teacher and see if you can find a solution.

SEVENTEEN

GUIDE TO CONVERSATION STARTER

"WELL BEGUN IS HALF DONE"

This is what applies to conversations too! The conversations that begin well mostly ends up as a great ones.

WHAT IS A CONVERSATION STARTER?

We face many situations in our life where several people surround us, and we wish to communicate/express ourselves or want to know about the other person. Still, we don't know precisely how to begin. A conversation starter is a phrase used for initiating conversations with known or unknown people in verbal form.

WHY DO WE NEED A CONVERSATION STARTER?

Most people are very comfortable in beginning casual conversations with people who are known to them or are their close associates. Still, when it comes to initiating one with strangers or people at work, they find it extremely challenging.

They have no idea about how to begin, what to start with, and keep thinking about how the other person will react. So here is a guide to some conversation starters that will help you to start a conversation effectively.

PARTIES

Parties are a great event to meet new people and socialize yourself. They are filled up with both well-known people as well as strangers. So, you need to approach people in a relevant cum nonformal manner.

HERE ARE SOME CONVERSATION STARTERS THAT CAN BE USED:

1. What kind of music do you like?
2. How do you know the host?
3. Have we met before?
4. The barbeque is really good, I think you should give it a try.
5. Have you tried this drink?
6. Do you like to dance?
7. Which game did you like the most?
8. Nice shoes/watch/purse, is it Puma/Rolex/ Lavie?
9. Have you heard about (any event)? Have you been here before?
10. How many people do you know here?
11. The food/music/games are really good, what do you think about it?
12. What drinks would you suggest?
13. What is your opinion about the ambience here?
14. What do you like the most, simple dinner parties or theme parties?

BUSINESS/CORPORATE EVENTS

Building relations is a necessary skill for anyone working in the corporate world. It affects both the personal and professional growth of an individual. Therefore it is important that you begin the conversation impressively

1. How did you start working in this company?
2. What did you think of the presentation?
3. How's the work environment in your firm?
4. Where did you get the inspiration for entrepreneurship?
5. Have you worked anywhere else before?
6. Have you attended any other conferences lately?
7. When are you planning to begin with the next project?
8. What do you think could have made the statistics better?
9. What is your opinion on the industry's progress this year?
10. How do you know about that firm? How did you get into this industry?
11. What do you think about the upcoming project?
12. Are you from Delhi?
13. What was the best part of this presentation according to you?
14. Have you ever been a host of any such conference?
15. How's work going for you?
16. How was your day at work today?
17. How's the XYZ project going?
18. Are you leading the XYZ project?
19. Are you Mr./Ms. ABC, the Vice President of XYZ?

STARTING CONVERSATIONS WITH A MUTUAL INTEREST

Conversations that include some common or shared interests are often very interesting, so if you have a mutual interest, you can approach by including it.

HERE ARE SOME CONVERSATION STARTERS THAT CAN BE USED:

1. What do you like to read, fiction, non-fiction, or sci-fi? [sci-fi: short form for science fiction]
2. Have you listened to any interesting podcasts lately?
3. What is your opinion on the XYZ movie? Do you like rock music?
4. This venue is great, isn't it?
5. What do you prefer, Apple or Android? Why?
6. What is the best sport to watch in your opinion?
7. Have you visited Himachal Pradesh?
8. Do you read any blogs?
9. It seems that you are quite interested in traveling, have you ever visited ABC?
10. Which team will lead the IPL this time?
11. Whom are you supporting? Mumbai Indians or Chennai Super kings?
12. Are you interested in watching horror movies?
13. I think it's high time that the government should amend this bill, what do you think?
14. Who is your favorite? Batman or Superman?
15. I think this movie is going to be a superhit, what is your opinion?
16. Are you from Jaipur? I have heard a lot about it's amazing puppet show!
17. Are you a tea or a coffee person?
18. Nice outfit. Is it from the Flora's?
19. Your opinions are very clear and unbiased, you seem to be a political analyst!
20. Your taste in clothes is very nice, do you work for the fashion industry?

CONVERSATION STARTERS FOR A DEEP CONVERSATION

Here are some conversation starters that can be used when you wish to have a deep conversation:

1. What are your long-term goals?
2. What are the top 3 things in your bucket list?
3. What is the best part of your life?
4. Do you have any regrets in your life?
5. What makes you the most happy?
6. Do you believe in God? Have you ever been in a dilemma?
7. What plans do you have for retirement? Whom do you consider as a mentor?
8. Who is the ideal personality you want to become like?
9. Who has influenced you the most in your life?
10. How do you keep yourself motivated? What is your opinion on success?
11. What principle do you follow in your life?
12. Do you miss the person you were back in your 20's?
13. What is your biggest dream in life?
14. What is your favorite hobby?
15. What is that one thing you cannot live without?
16. What mischiefs did you often do as a child?
17. What do you think the world will be like in 10 years from now?

CONVERSATION STARTERS WITH KIDS

Here are some conversation starters that can be used to have a conversation with kids:

1. Which class do you study in?
2. What is your favorite subject at school?

3. Which is your dream destination to visit? What's your favorite cartoon character?
4. Which game do you love to play?
5. Do you like indoor games or outdoor games?
6. What is the best part that you like about your parents?
7. Who is your best friend?
8. Do you like pets?
9. Which animal would you like to keep as a pet?
10. What do you wish to become when you grow up?
11. Do you believe in Aliens?
12. What is your favorite TV show?
13. What are your hobbies?
14. I think you have a sweet tooth.
15. Which is your favorite play garden?
16. Which toys do you love to play with?
17. Who is your favorite superhero?

Thank You!

Thank You! Before you go, I'd like to say "thank you" again for purchasing my book. I know you could have picked from dozens of books on this topic, but you took a chance with my system and that means a lot to me. So a BIG THANKS for Purchasing this book and reading all the way to the end. Now I'd like to ask for a "SMALL" favor. Please take a minute or two and leave a review for this book on Amazon.This feedback will greatly help me continue writing the kind of books that will help you get the results you've dreamed of and more. And if you love it, then let me know! I would be forever grateful to hear from you!!!